This or That Pets

Is a RABBIT or a GUINEA PIG the Pet for Me?

by Mari Schuh

PEBBLE
a capstone imprint

Published by Pebble, an imprint of Capstone
1710 Roe Crest Drive, North Mankato, Minnesota 56003
capstonepub.com

Library of Congress Cataloging-in-Publication Data is available on the Library of Congress website.
ISBN: 9780756579036 (hardcover)
ISBN: 9780756578985 (paperback)
ISBN: 9780756578992 (ebook PDF)

Summary: Rabbits and guinea pigs are cute, furry, and fun! But which one would make the best pet for you? Which one needs more space? Which one lives longer? Which one is cleaner? Compare these two amazing pets side by side to see which might be your perfect pet!

Image Credits
Alamy: Janet Horton, 13; Getty Images: Alice Wanwarameth, 14, Carol Yepes, 9, 19, PeopleImages, 17, Roberto, 6; Shutterstock: Alexander_Safonov, 15, Andrii Oleksiienko, 7, Arlee.P, 21, David Prado Perucha, 11, Denys Kurbatov, Cover (top), EZ-Stock Studio, 8, Lipatova Maryna, 12, Mary Swift, 4, Mateusz Sienkiewicz, 16, Natasha Pankina, background (throughout), Pixel-Shot, 18, Radek Havlicek, 5, Rita_Kochmarjova, 10, SashkaB, Cover (bottom), Wirestock Creators, 20

Editorial Credits
Editor: Carrie Sheely; Designer: Bobbie Nuytten; Media Researcher: Jo Miller; Production Specialist: Whitney Schaefer

Dedication: For Pedro, Karma, Kindle, and Nola

Printed and bound in China.   PO 5834

Table of Contents

Words in **bold** are in the glossary.

Getting a New Pet

Fluffy ears. Soft fur. Chubby cheeks.
Rabbits and guinea pigs are cute and fun!
These pets have some things in common.
But they also have some differences.
Find out which pet might be better for you!

Small or Big Home

Rabbits and guinea pigs usually live in a cage or **hutch**. It's better to have the cage or hutch inside a home instead of outdoors. Rabbits are bigger animals. They need a bigger cage or hutch.

Both pets need to spend time out of their cage or hutch every day. The space needed for this time needs to be bigger for rabbits. Around four hours a day is best.

Cheap or Costly

Which pet costs more money? It depends. There are many **breeds** of guinea pigs and rabbits. Some might need to go to a **veterinarian** more often than others. Rabbits can cost more. They usually live longer than guinea pigs.

Owners need to buy food and supplies for their rabbits and guinea pigs. These pets eat hay, pellets, and fresh vegetables. Rabbits tend to eat more. Both pets need **bedding** and toys too.

Quiet or Loud

Squeak! Grunt! Guinea pigs make loud noises! Rabbits are quiet pets. They like their homes to be quiet too. Rabbits might make soft sounds.

Clean or Messy

Rabbits and guinea pigs **groom** themselves. But owners also need to groom their pets. Rabbits should be brushed at least twice a week. Guinea pigs with short coats need brushing at least once a week. Those with long coats need grooming many times a week.

Guinea pig cages can get messy! They poop and pee often. They also kick and throw bedding and hay. Rabbits can be trained to use a **litter box** easier than guinea pigs. This can help keep their hutches clean.

Cuddly or Not

It can be fun to hold and cuddle a pet. But not all pets enjoy it. Most rabbits do not like to be picked up. They might scratch, kick, or bite. Rabbits feel safer when their feet are on the floor.

Many guinea pigs are okay with being gently held. Some like to cuddle and be petted.

Friendly or Shy

Guinea pigs are very **social**. They play with people and other guinea pigs. Guinea pigs do well when they live with another guinea pig.

Each rabbit has its own **personality**. Some rabbits tend to be **shy**. They hop away from people. Other rabbits are friendly. They hop to people. They like being petted.

Short or Long Lives

Pets are a lot of fun! But having a pet is a big **responsibility**. Why? Pets can live a long time. Guinea pigs often live four to eight years. Pet rabbits can live eight to 12 years.

Which Pet Is Best for You?

There is no perfect pet. Every pet is different. So is every family! The best pet for you might not be the best pet for your friend. This activity can help you find out which pet might be best for you.

What You Need:

- pencil or pen
- notebook or piece of paper

What You Do:

1. Read the Table of Contents of this book. Write the Table of Contents words in your notebook. Use the words to make two columns. For example, for the entry "Quiet or Loud," write the word "Quiet" in the first column. Then write the word "Loud" in the second column.

2. Think about how important each item is to you. For each entry, circle the word that would work best for you and your family. For example, would you be bothered by a pet that is loud? Would you need a pet that is always quiet?

3. When you are done reviewing each entry, read the book again. How many of your circled words describe guinea pigs? How many of your circled words describe rabbits? The pet with the higher total might be better for you.

Glossary

bedding (BED-ing)—materials used to make an animal's bed or litter box

breed (BREED)—a certain kind of animal within an animal group

groom (GROOM)—to keep clean

hutch (HUTCH)—a pet's home

litter box (LIT-ur BOX)—a container indoors for a pet to go to the bathroom

personality (pur-suh-NAL-uh-tee)—all of the qualities or traits that make an animal different

responsibility (ri-spon-suh-BIL-uh-tee)—a duty or a job

shy (SHYE)—not feeling comfortable around people

social (SOH-shuhl)—wanting to be near people or animals

veterinarian (vet-ur-uh-NER-ee-uhn)—a doctor trained to take care of animals

Read More

Greenwood, Nancy. *My Pet Rabbit*. New York: Gareth Stevens Publishing, 2023.

Shofner, Melissa Raé. *Is a Rabbit a Good Pet for Me?* New York: PowerKids Press, 2020.

Thielges, Alissa. *Curious About Guinea Pigs*. Mankato, MN: Amicus, 2023.

Internet Sites

20 Fun Facts About Guinea Pigs!
guineapigmagazine.com/20-fun-facts-about-guinea-pigs

National Geographic Kids: 10 Hopping Fun Rabbit Facts!
natgeokids.com/uk/discover/animals/general-animals/10-hopping-fun-rabbit-facts

Ranger Rick: Watch a Guinea Pig "Popcorning"
rangerrick.org/rr_videos/watch-a-guinea-pig-popcorning

Index

About the Author

Mari Schuh's love of reading began with cereal boxes at the kitchen table. Today she is the author of hundreds of nonfiction books for beginning readers. Mari lives in the Midwest with her husband and their sassy house rabbit. Learn more about her at marischuh.com.